I0188086

ENDLESS
TEACHABLE MOMENTS

An Expression on the Art and Education of Sport

Jason Aron Ronai

Copyright © 2022 by ETM PRESS, Chicago, IL
An imprint of ENDLESS TEACHABLE MOMENTS, LLC

First published in the United States of America

All rights reserved. No portion of this book may be
reproduced in any form without permission in writing from the
publisher, except the use of quotations in a book review and
as permitted by U.S. copyright law. Thank you for buying an
authorized edition of this book. For permissions, contact
ETM PRESS.

Book Cover and Design by Satori
Edited by Evelyn Asher

ENDLESS TEACHABLE MOMENTS
An Expression on the Art and Education of Sport
Jason Aron Ronai
ISBN: 978-0-578-31661-1 (hardback)
ISBN: 979-8-9852647-6-0 (paperback)
ISBN: 979-8-9852647-0-8 (ebook)
Library of Congress Control Number: 2022901124

1st Edition

Publisher: ETM PRESS

To Mama and Dad

Poetically defined, a teachable moment is an occurrence of

educational potential and value. It is a choice, a response,

a result, or a circumstance through which an applicable life-value

can be absorbed or taught in the moment and/or reflected

upon in the years to come.

CONTENTS

PURPOSE

There were approximately one hundred and fifty coaches waiting for me to begin the seminar. I walked slowly, gazing around the room, assuredly, waiting for just enough uncomfortable silence. I then posed the question, *why do you coach?* I paused again, took a few more silent steps, raised my head and repeated, *why do you coach?*

It's a question we must ask as coaches. It's a question that requires deep thought and an answer. For parents, you are all educators. You should ask and answer this question for yourself. For athletes reading this book, answer for yourself, *why am I an athlete?*

I read my "why" to the coaches word for word:

I coach because sport is art. It is good, beautiful, and complex.

I coach because there is winning and losing and we must learn

to overcome both.

I coach because sport surfaces the inner soul of an athlete – their

truest form.

I coach because sport provides endless teachable moments.

* * *

I crafted this book to be good art - a painting that remains on the wall, no matter the times. I hope it ignites deep thought and wisdom each time it is consumed.

Writing this poetic memoir became necessary the more I felt athletes needed one of their own to create an expression - a literary companion with a mentor's approach. The inner soul of an evolved athlete is revealed on each page, affirming the low-lit flame that permanently resides inside the heart of nearly every athlete and coach reading this book. My intention is to expand familial and societal thinking on the journey of sport.

We owe it to the younger generation of athletes to embrace and promote the art and education of the journey. When athletes are equipped to absorb the values of sport, they are empowered to detach from the outcome. Sport is a beautiful immersion; a deep and lasting friendship.

I've been a teacher and a coach. Coaching is gold for the educator who seeks teaching mastery. Values are ever present, but sport consistently tests those values in unpredictable ways. As a coach, I make a point to proactively study and seek the teachable moments, to never let them drift away. Moreover, I seek continuous growth in recognition of the teachable moment. The moments can be advanced or basic, but they never fail to be plentiful - a daily feast for the comprehensive educator. We must love growth to seek advanced teaching moments and we must love discipline to address the basic, time and again. And in addressing the teachable moments, we must aim to fine-tune the art of delivery in each lesson we give, no matter how many times we must repeat the theme of the common message in the common moment. Sounds like teaching. Sounds like leadership. Sounds like parenting. Sounds like discipline. Sounds like love.

I believe athletes of all ages desire to express their undefined and often misunderstood love of sport. We yearn to be untamed in our expression. You see extreme facial expressions - unparalleled excitement and sometimes, despair - on athletes during sport. Yet this emotion exists nowhere else in their life.

Athletes have a passion; an urge; a curiosity; a rare intensity; a unique set of human emotions displayed during the complex fusion of fun, competition, and team-accountability. Perhaps this poetic memoir — a trailhead — will inspire the artists within to go forward with self-expression in writing, painting, or song. My hope is that these pages will inspire leaders to create space for artistic expression.

On a more personal note, sport was a dear, loyal friend to me during an experience of unthinkable tragedy in my youth, providing me with an outlet, a community, a structure, and a vision that helped carry me through. The expression of that experience on the pages ahead continues to carry me through.

As you read, you'll hear a young ballplayer's voice, the dreamer. You'll see through the teary eyes of the retired athlete, revisiting ball fields and meanings of the past. You'll meet an emboldened coach, a teacher, a leader, an artist, or a combination of all four. Each character, a teammate in the harmonious expression of the moments that matter most when our playing days begin and when they bid us farewell.

There are twenty-four poems in this book for a reason. If you know you know.

Drink each poem very slowly, perhaps a daily sip and reflection.

I sincerely hope you are moved by at least one.

INTRODUCTION
BEYOND THE TRAILHEAD OF SPORT

A trailhead marks the beginning. Often, a trailhead is a nondescript wooden post etched with the title of a soon-to-be path created by a team of earth, creatures, humans, and time. Symbolic, it's the point where one steps forward, then beyond. Each trail is authentic to you. The weather from years, months, weeks, or even minutes prior, creates an original path - for you. In essence, the trail is your journey, *your* choice today. The journey will never be the same for another. Honor it with your presence and mindfulness, step by step.

Sport is a journey. It is a special and intimate process for the athlete, both child and adult. It holds a dear place in the heart. Each journey of sport carves an authentic trail. Each has a beginning - its own wooden post trailhead, most often a childhood moment which remains etched in the athlete's mind as the source of our original infatuation. It's that rite of passage that serves as a key link to the distancing relationship we have with our child selves. We step forward, beyond the trailhead when we slip our small hand into a first padded, leather ball glove, open the gym doors and smell the finish of creaky wood floors at a first practice, locate and gaze at our team name on our first season schedule handed to us by our first coach, see our original number on the back of a fresh, official team jersey. Are we five years of age? Seven? Twelve?

My first moment — the first step beyond the trailhead — was the unfolding of a baseball jersey, and its scent of new and official. *Like the big leaguers*, I mused. I was six years old. My family lived in Mars Hill, North Carolina. My baseball jersey number was two.

The trail of sport is unpredictable, curious, rigorous, wild - exhilarating. The trail is *fun*, in the most and least sophisticated sense of the word. Sport, like a natural trail, is directly or indirectly empowering, not without obstacles to overcome. The obstacles are ever evolving and beautiful - roots, steep hills, slopes, treacherous terrain, all which provide as much beauty and art as they do challenge. The outcome is unclear as it is in most of life's travels. Thus, the trail of the sport experience becomes a journey of endless teachable moments, if we, the guardians, let the trail be what it was meant to be.

Poetically defined, a teachable moment is an occurrence of educational potential and value. A choice, a response, a result, or a circumstance through which an applicable life-value can be absorbed or taught in the moment or reflected upon in the years to come.

Athletes may, on occasion, recognize the value of the present teachable moment and apply that knowledge to their path's obstacles and future choices. That is the hope, but not always the expectation. Wisdom requires years of proper distilling. Most often, the values-based education born in that one moment is chosen and delivered, or not, by the leader - the coach, the parent, the invested family member, the community of educators, those that may have assisted the child's first step beyond the trailhead and onto the path.

The chosen values of sport empower the teachable moments, and vice versa. There are many. Values are a precious and delicate choice. The internal discipline to educate in the moment may be a leader's greatest hurdle and fear.

May we all grow in our values, holding dear the choices we make when the teachable moment arrives. May we be ready and willing, as they occur before, during, and after competition. May we seek the moments, and may we seek to grow in our educational application of those moments while the athlete innocently navigates the trail ahead, which they originally choose, mind you, because sport is fun and friends are there to share the experience – a fact backed by research.

The trail of sport has mechanisms. Sport mechanisms are plentiful, as are the values that may grow from them. Practice is an educational mechanism of sport, which, in proper use, may lead us to a growth-mindset. The mechanism of competition may lead to humility. The mechanism of sportsmanship may lead to integrity or empathy or respect, and so on and so on. All sport mechanisms have the opportunity to build values, but are incumbent on an adult leader who chooses to be an educator before becoming a winner or a loser.

The end of the trail is different for all of us. Inevitably, it's a reflective journey back to the beginning. There are achievement pinnacles and value pinnacles that define and conclude the journey. These are the peaks that rise above the clouds or the open prairie at the end of the wood - the end of the trail.

Some get to the achievement pinnacle, an end result where winning, accolades, scholarship, and profession live. Winning is splendid. It's okay to love to win, to want to win, and to loathe losing. Accolades, scholarship, and professional sports are amazing and desirable feats as well. But most athletes don't make it there. However, we all have the trail. Each of us experiences an authentic journey of the trail in which value pinnacles are abundant. We have access to that education. And what is it we take from the incredible journey that is unique to us? What lessons do we learn along the way? These are the questions we continuously contemplate. If we pay attention, the answer gets better and better through the years.

I don't fault myself or anyone else that aimed for the achievement peak, the one of accolade, scholarship, and profession through sport. My imagination still runs wild up there. But too early of a focus on achievement may impact our original intent - to play a game with friends, have fun, and learn much about life along the way. An unhealthy focus on the outcome can stunt growth. It can change us and those around us. We are, in fact, only human. We are not immune to the poisons.

The poisons are ego, arrogance, and greed. Damaging poisons, all mostly built from the insecurity of wounded adults. Not com- pletely irreversible but those species of pride push the limit. They cause us to veer off the trail. The community of adults can, if we choose, keep the athlete persisting toward the value pinnacle by methodically learning, accentuating, modeling, and applying the educational moments that encapsulate the trail. It is imperative we disconnect from the outcome in order to absorb the art, education, and beauty of the journey. Sport is good and beautiful. Art exists on the trail.

Unpredictable adversity, raw emotion, and love coexist on the trail. Expression, culture, mindfulness, strategy, and a language children understand - all exist on the journey of sport. The trail, not the result, is education in its most innocent form.

In years of reflection, I've found my trail important enough to bestow it with words and title. I've named it *Beech Glen Trail*, the baseball field of my youth, where I met sport at a time I most needed it. It still exists, I think, in Mars Hill, North Carolina. But if it is gone or repurposed, it remains in my memories as it was. I do hope Beech Glen has been preserved, as all fields of grass, dirt, play, and joy should. It's time for my soul to revisit.

There is an inscription on my trailhead that defines all that I learned from my journey. It reads:

<u>Beech Glen Trail</u>

Collect from this journey the endless teachable moments.

Return them not, but return.

There is winning and losing, and we must overcome both.

Be relentless in the pursuit of figuring it out.

Be great, break barriers, honor the struggle, discern the good art.

And let love get you through.

What is the inscription on your trailhead?

Write it down, even just a draft. Honor the journey with your words.

ENDLESS TEACHABLE MOMENTS

In your wiser years, you'll respect the leader who mustered the courage to consistently address the teachable moment, and, as consequence of wisdom, you'll resent the leader who didn't.

EMPTY BLEACHERS

A person may say, *I take great interest in theater*.

Society shines them in a sophisticated light.

I take great interest in symphony. Same light.

I take great interest in sport — seems fanatical.

The sophisticated light moves away from sport,

Undeservingly lower in the intellectual hierarchy.

I take great interest in the art of sport.

The art! Yes. The art of sport.

This changes the view.

Sit next to me on empty bleachers.

Close your eyes.

Visualize the theater. Hear the symphony.

Sport, when viewed as artform,

Expands human relationships.

Minds open, hearts empathize, limits change.

An unbounded, soulful bonding.

Oh, poetry, we naturally bond.

We shut the door to life's noise.

We walk with words - breathing them.

The poetry of sport deserves no less.

When words gift themselves to you,

Gift them a proper setting in return.

A warm fireplace and the good chair,

The hideaway café,

The iron bench near water,

The base of a hugging weeping willow,

Empty ball field bleachers during golden hour.

Any tree, ballfield, or good chair

That gives you mindful company,

And absorbs the words with you.

Wherever life takes you,

Let child-mind and child-soul follow.

Be courageous in softening your heart

To words that evoke memories

Of the innocence of a childhood moment

You long to experience again.

FLOURISH

A child - once us -

Chooses sport for two reasons:

It's fun, and friends are there.

And this is not opinion.

Along the way, an athlete discovers sport

To be a great and loyal friend,

A listener who provides solace,

A trusted companion always there.

Sport intends on great friendship

With all of the arriving children,

But, sport, despite its great power and might

Must overcome one grand obstacle:

The adults who forge the environment

Where that friendship flourishes or perishes.

The art of sport lies in the human connection of purposeful, coordinated, strategic movement, and the expression of raw human emotion that emanates from the success or failure of this moment.

ON FEARING
THE TEACHABLE MOMENT

Educators of great and little acumen,

Of great and little experience,

Of great and little resume,

Share, consequently, the same human fear.

This common fear fills like water rising,

When the teachable moment occurs,

When it comes face to face.

A fear that their teaching will be rejected

Or wildly unpopular for a second,

And that conflict will not feel good,

For all the personal reasons.

So, they pause, letting the teachable moment float away.

Responsibility drifts off,

Unable to return

To disrupt the safer shores of momentary silence.

They convince themselves of why –

A series of sophisticated excuses,

Perhaps blaming the system,

Or the child.

One decision to look the other way,

Keeps the educator from joining the outliers

Who took a chance at failing

Or succeeding,

And being exactly what the student needed,

Despite the momentary discomfort

Of being authentic, in an authentic moment,

Vulnerable, in a vulnerable moment.

So, don't be so afraid

Of people, or decisions, or discomfort, or yourself.

SURROUNDED BY POETRY

It became clear

In the musings of my older years

That through a lifetime in sport,

I was surrounded, all along, by poetry.

Sport is a world of artful theater -

An imagination that houses unpredictable storylines,

Endless teachable moments.

And for some, like me, a world that begs to unfold on paper.

Never underestimate

The power of moments,

Theatrical and educational,

In the life of an athlete.

May we be humble enough

To never dismiss

The art and expression of sport

In the soul of a child.

Rather, let us celebrate

The heart of the child,

A heart surrounded by poetry

That best remains, forever, in the athlete.

AND SO WE FLEE

These words - music in my soul,

Dormant, once vibrant, waiting impatiently.

Words influenced by dear people.

Tragedy, too, and its own language.

Sparked from moments through coaches,

And my father, the coach.

Dad's teams, my idols and eventual purpose.

My teams with forever-connected hearts.

Like me, the words were ready to rise

From the ashes of a journey with sport.

That dear ol' loyal friend - sport.

A friend that replaced my brother's presence,

He, so close to me in age and connection,

Took his final breath, suddenly, right before my eyes.

That image, an old tattered film in my mind.

So, I and we - the children - flee to sports, music, and words.

Encourage art and sport early.

Help intertwine their relationship with children.

Especially the children who choose art or sport or both

To help overcome the unthinkable.

A single competition is the grandest educator. Competition

supplies adversity, reveals character, challenges attitude,

and offers a myriad of choices in how we respond. Regardless of

outcome, choose to learn and grow.

LIFE'S PRE-GAME SPEECH

This is your pre-game speech for life.

A message you mustn't forget.

Do only your very best.

Be honestly prepared. Render no regret.

Your very best is thick-skinned effort

Grown of trials and unbreakable core.

Be poised, resilient, and by all means

Get right back up, off the floor.

Make no mistake of comparison.

There's only your mirror's view.

You'll dance the internal victory.

Competing as the best version of you.

TO BE SHARED WITH FRIENDS

When tempted by money in the game,

Motivation for sport may cease to be the same.

The temptation of prestige, a poison eerily strong.

When no longer resisted, the purity will be gone.

Remember your *why-*

Before sport becomes means to an end -

That sport is just plain fun,

Meant to be shared with friends.

NELSON

You don't believe in the power of sport.

You can't or won't approach the window of thought.

Nonessential. Extra. Budget-sucking. Barbaric. Cute.

Not part of the larger intellectual discussion.

Seems fun for them, you think, but you don't know them.

You know you, and your circle,

And that's all you think you need.

I gave you my name, but my name is not Nelson.

Though I wish, in that moment, my name was, Nelson.

You'd listen to Nelson. I did. But I am not him.

Then, I told you my life's work -

The art, education, and culture of sport.

The Endless Teachable Moments thing, you hear.

Though I followed it, more eloquently, with my words.

To me, sport is:

> *a physical, competitive, critical thinking mechanism*
>
> *with applicable life values and social emotional impact*
>
> *involving a team or individual that partake*
>
> *in often rigorous, diverse, strategic movements*
>
> *requiring mental, emotional, and physical*
>
> *preparation, growth, and aptitude.*

Sport empowers. Period.

But you only heard,

The Endless Teachable Moments thing.

Because my name is not Nelson.

I spoke again, trying to capture your mind,

Not for my gain but on behalf of kids and coaches,

I transported you to that little-known place my mind travels

to each day -

That bench on the baseball field at Beech Glen,

That lives in my wondrous mind

As the place of good art and purity of my childhood,

Where my father hit me ground balls.

I declared, *but let me tell you more, good sir,*

You smiled, condescendingly,

Perched on your frail intellectual tower,

Built by you, and elitism, and arrogance, and society,

From fragile bricks of bias and academic accolade.

Follow me if you can, good sir, I tempted.

Grandest voice, I commanded, *SPORT HAS THE POWER!*

I paused, for effect, then continued, *to change the world.*

> *Sport has the power to inspire,*
>
> *It has the power to unite people in a way that little else does.*
>
> *It speaks to youth in a language they understand.*

It can create hope, where there was once only despair.

It is more powerful than governments in breaking down

racial barriers.

It laughs in the face of all types of discrimination.

Sport is the game of lovers.

Again, I paused, poised, not doubting the words

But holding onto them, steadfastly.

For one should not walk away from one's words.

You can't deny the power of those words, I declared.

But in my heart, I know, you denied the power of me.

My name is not Nelson.

Perched, still, you commended the words,

An accepting nod and stare,

Pivoting to the incomplete question, *okay?*

You allowed my words in your narrow intellectual door,

But your perch is comfortable, where I am not easily invited.

My name is not Nelson.

Instead, I invited you to that place

Of good art and purity.

Beech Glen, the ball field of my youthful soul,

Where the children are the most sophisticated in the park.

I must tell you, good sir, those are not my words.

Those words belong to Nelson. And surely my name is not Nelson.

From your perch, you look down and ask, *Nelson? Nelson who?*

I smiled and uttered, *Mandela. Nelson Mandela.*

He chose those words, and I simply repeated.

I walked slowly away.

You then slipped down from the perch and chose to follow me.

And Mandela's wisdom.

For the kids and coaches, whose world is sport,

I am not too prideful, good sir,

To let you through my intellectual door.

Good leaders establish core values for their team.

Transformative leaders create an educational culture

where the team learns

to hold accountable the values they set for themselves.

SEE MY ART

My true expression –

That which emerges on hardwood,

You haven't seen it, or me.

Dear teacher, you see fragments.

I'm here, in the classroom - I want to be here.

Not whole, though, only a partial version.

You don't know me. Or my art.

You speak of the great paintings.

Song. It moves you.

The thrill of the theater, you say.

You do absorb poetry, YOUR poetry.

Intellectual sophistication, you yearn.

Are you sophisticated enough to recognize my art?

Like the painter I practice,

I use inspiration to create.

In my studio, the arena.

But I'm an athlete.

No, never JUST an athlete.

Can your view of me evolve?

You've never asked. Never about my art.

I invite you to my quiet studio.

Me, gym floor, and ball.

Observe my practice, my canvas.

My palette, all the colors, and choices.

My art - an expression of movement and coordination.

Peak through the window of my studio.

What might you find in me?

Here, the gym, a young artist,

Reveals his true and vulnerable soul.

An expression you thought didn't live.

I am an athlete. I feel whole in my studio.

My full expression of self, the one you desire, is here.

No different than an instrumental introvert

You and others deem *quiet genius.*

My body is my instrument.

Listen to the cello in your mind

As you watch me move.

Perhaps your eyes will open wide.

I am an athlete.

One that craves to share his art with you,

So that we can begin to educate one another.

PROMISE TO RISE

(dedicated to my parents)

Through the unimaginable days

You stayed near and present.

And taught me to rise.

Each season -

The unthinkable and the glorious ones -

I rose as you rose.

You coached me, each differently

The point, though, you coached me.

Choosing love and resilience over despair.

Near worthy of theater, our family,

Against the steep grade and tragic terrain

Of the unsolicited, arduous mountain we've climbed.

I promised you I'd rise,

Each morning, just get back up and seek light,

No matter the darkness of many yesterdays.

Today, I present a promise kept.

A sunrise of words

In clearer, softer, Carolina-blue skies.

WIN THIS DAY

Walk steadfast and tall through this door,

The challenge will soon take place.

Beautiful, inevitable, internal confrontation

Between you and mirror, face to face.

Approach with arrogance, the game will grin.

Cling to ego, the game will win.

Arrive apathetic, passive, disengaged —

Just turn back. Do not dare come in.

Leave such poisons at the door,

Our daily journey shall begin.

The grand table we set for teammates,

A mighty feast of growth within.

Shallow be the focus on outcomes

Or what others think you to be about.

Be relentless, be present, in pursuit of poise.

And the process of figuring it out.

The mirror, run to it.

Gaze long at your truth today.

Give up social thrones,

Unlock the competitor's soul.

Commit to win this day.

SPORT IS EVERY ART

Sport is movement.

Like dance.

Synchronized, but sometimes free-form.

Unpredictable, graceful, coordinated, chaotic at times.

Distantly choreographed by rules and coaches.

Evolving, like the human brain and body.

Sport is theater.

Physical expression. Emotional cleansing,

Loosely scripted by strategy and talent,

Without prewritten ending, it remains a performance,

Drenched with drama, comedy, and passion.

Sport is a painting.

A canvas of earth and human tones.

The picturesque venues will still your mind and soul.

A masterpiece, from street lot to sandlot,

From Kentucky bluegrass to hardwood.

Sport is music.

The sounds of sport live in us, like song.

Voices, ricochets, nature, joy, pain, breath.

Familiar family voices, whistles, echoes,

And the cello of triumph and defeat.

Sport is architecture.

Victory sculpted by science,

Constructed by an imperfect blueprint

Of strategy, of structure, of hope.

Standing tall and firm through the storms of society.

Sport is a nonfiction novel.

Narrative upon narrative,

Driven by societal admiration and internal fire.

You are an author of your athletic journey,

But so too is the game.

Sport is good and beautiful art.

Let us all be sophisticated and childlike

To drink it slowly into our soul.

There is much written on how we overcome defeat.

More advanced, it seems to me, is the person who learns ever so quickly

to overcome the complexities of victory.

BLENDED COLORS

(intermission)

A yearning for societal unity

And positive discourse

Remains no different than centuries prior.

In divided times, if ever there are none,

Sport persists with an unfinished canvas.

Ever-evolving, abstract unity of blended colors.

Elegantly stated by Nelson Mandela

A point no athletic commoner could sell:

Sport has the power to change the world.

It has the power to inspire.

It has the power to unite people in a way little else does.

It speaks to youth in a language they understand.

Sport can create hope where once there was only despair.

Empathy and love - yes, empathy and love

Exist at the beginning, middle, and end of competition.

Peacefully, they coexist with tenacity and toughness.

Never, as the opposite of competitiveness.

Competition requires a unity of blended colors,

As does victory.

SPORT RISING

Social. Emotional. Learning.

Popular culture. Cultural responsiveness.

Warriors of the educational rising.

Yet we always had sport. Yes, sport. Just, sport.

Sitting there, forever waiting to be useful.

A connected universal language all its own.

Tired of being, also, a misunderstood *only*.

Sport - sophisticated, intellectual, diverse,

Responsive, rigorous, unpredictable,

Nonconforming, mindful,

Waiting to be heard and seen.

Waiting, perhaps beyond its own lifetime.

Until the world gains the necessary emotional intelligence.

But sport is not heard.

The self-crowned, intellectually elite may dismiss it.

Therefore sport - like it does in the tough -

Gets back up, rising off the ground resolutely

Until its genius is acknowledged

As a necessary warrior in the educational rising.

THE GOOD ART

I've found the good art resides on the wall,

Fitting perfectly, where eyes are drawn, felt by all.

Like the great concepts of the great coaches,

Survivors of time and the tumult of trendy, narrow approaches.

Universally created with timeless application,

Void of cowardice construct for the elite population.

Tis' the educator's great opus and trace

A timeless concept of blended colors, all colors can embrace.

The good art resides on the wall.

Methodically brushed into blank canvas,

Courageously painted for all.

Simple though it may seem, sport's greatest teachable moment

occurs when we realize the improvement

made in a single competition was a result of multiple

days of rigorous practice in our alone time.

VALUE PINNACLES

This is for parents and coaches.

Absorb these words with intention.

You have the power to educate.

You have influence beyond mention.

A child has two motivations to begin the trail of sport:

Because it's fun. Because friends are there.

The trailhead reads: *abundant purity and joy.*

Fun, friendship, original youthful care.

Adulterated pinnacles may soon interfere.

Poisons of ego and accolade seep through.

Let the child's innocent motivations prevail

While you empower pinnacles of value.

Endless teachable moments.

This trail blooms values-based education.

Let sport develop its natural self.

Let life values be your motivation.

With *abundant purity and joy* as the trailhead.

And life values the pinnacle or peak,

Learn the natural mechanisms of sport,

Then choose the values you seek.

The mechanisms of sport are ever present,

Regularly convening.

It's the understanding of their potential value

That gives a sport its true meaning.

Practice is a mechanism.

Its pinnacle value is industriousness.

Teamwork, also a mechanism,

May lead an athlete to selflessness.

Expression is a sport mechanism.

Underappreciated by educators throughout.

It may lead to mindfulness,

A value adults can't do without.

We experience the leadership of coaches,

A mechanism with many diverse voices.

The value of consciousness then develops.

A child's list of heroes grows choices.

The most vital sport mechanism

Comes through the great educator: competition.

And in overcoming all the wins and losses,

The value of poise may come to fruition.

The list of mechanisms and values is endless.

The journey of sport provides that canvas.

How you choose to paint it with the child

Is what will influence their value stanzas.

Abundant purity and joy remains the trailhead.

I'll have it until the very end.

Adults allowed sport to teach me,

And sport became a lifelong friend.

CREATE THE STRUGGLE

Where world-class and genius bloom

Be not just luck or blessed child.

The greats rise from special harvest

Of habit-seeds in a field growing wild.

A distracted harvester blooms stale crop.

Apathetic seasons, weeds, droughts, complaining.

While a focused-tending blooms the great habit of practice -

Deep, consistent, rigorous training.

UNSCRIPTED

Wisdom and life-experience converge,

A gathering of respected friends.

Certainty flows in their banter,

Of what is good and beautiful.

We are certain about sport.

Competition involving coordination

Of body and mind.

We are certain this is good.

Competition involving the fusion

Of joy and emotion,

Physical expression.

We are certain this is beautiful.

Competition involving the togetherness

Of community, discerning and meeting obstacles.

Unscripted endings and friends.

We are certain this is good.

When defeat happens — because it will —

one's search for cause should begin and end at the mirror.

YOU AND THE BALL

Young athlete,

The source of our motivation,

Often a common mental miscue,

That the daily battle you think you face,

Is against the uniformed opponent — untrue.

Best you evolve your thinking now,

For the fiercest battle of all,

Is relentlessly and endlessly internal,

It's you versus you, and the ball.

FADEAWAY

Math part of playing ball?

Number sense. Hmm.

Scoreboards, deficits, margins.

Statistics!

I just want to play ball.

That doesn't mean I don't want to learn.

Science in playing ball?

Physics. Hmm.

Trajectories, angles, elements.

Velocity and degrees.

Yes! Every time I shoot or throw.

Teach me. Connect them.

I connect them, somewhat.

Reading in playing ball?

I like reading.

Articles, recaps.

Strategy!

Poems.

But mostly I just want to play ball.

Perhaps more than I want to read.

Can I just read about playing ball?

As long as I read a lot?

I do read a lot about ball.

More than I read fiction.

Culture, language, and art in playing ball?

Expression, adaptation.

Community!

We can learn much from playing ball.

We. Hmm.

What if more teachers played ball?

They'd learn a thing or two.

About playing ball.

And the genius of sport.

About me!

About their own understanding

Of why I just want to play ball.

Of my fadeaway, here and there.

TRAGIC

Tragic, the spirit of a kid -

Floating away -

On a raft that eventually will sink.

The kid had all the talent,

All the tools,

All the perceived gifts,

Even if exaggerated, slightly,

By the clingers and the crowd.

But not one coach

Throughout the kid's life

Chose to swim

To the child in the sinking raft.

To inspire dedication,

Harvest accountability,

Follow through as a mentor.

Protect.

Or teach continuous growth within.

The child could swim, you see,

Away from the sinking raft,

And back to land,

But simply did not know it.

The poison that divides a child from a great friendship with sport

is assembled from prestige, power, and ego, which of course,

is a poison mostly concocted by wounded adults.

THE GREATEST TEACHER

In my wild ride with sport,

I've concluded the most teachable moments

Exist within the adversity of a single competition.

Winning and losing,

We must learn to overcome both,

Often together.

And we must repeat this practice time and again.

The next time

We rise to meet competition

Where we are,

Equipped, ill-equipped,

Depending on our choices

During and after the adversity.

Similar, I think, to life

And the choices we make every day.

EIGHT AND TWENTY-FOUR

Briefly, we breathed his new art.

He'd only begun to create.

On the brink, he was, of his own genre.

Sadly, true genius lived in number eight.

Future wisdom was lost when we lost him.

A new universe, he founded as an artist.

He was the rare and beautiful bean,

Growing into a rare and beautiful harvest.

Societal perceptions began to alter,

He was influencing a new worldview.

That sport is a soulful art form.

And the athlete, an artist too.

His brazen creativity was without limit.

He opened a more sophisticated door

For a rising generation of athletes,

Who needn't suppress their art anymore.

For every new painting rising in the arena,

Every new poem born of sweat on a gym floor,

We honor his art and masterpieces unrevealed.

We carry the torch for twenty-four.

OLD FRIEND

And to sport, I'm forever grateful.

You surrounded my soul with art,

And poetry, culture, and endless teachable moments.

You gave me a language I understood.

I have yet to learn all you have to offer,

But once again, on these pages,

Our friendship has flourished.

When athletes complete their final game, what remains

are memories, moments, and the values learned along the way.

There will be a teachable moment today.

Capture it.

www.ingramcontent.com/pod-product-compliance
Lightning Source LLC
Chambersburg PA
CBHW031932090426
42811CB00002B/154